50 Farm-To-Table Recipes for Home

By: Kelly Johnson

Table of Contents

- Roasted Vegetable Frittata
- Spinach and Kale Salad with Fresh Berries
- Grilled Zucchini and Tomato Skewers
- Lemon Herb Roast Chicken
- Quinoa-Stuffed Bell Peppers
- Garlic and Herb Mashed Potatoes
- Butternut Squash Soup with Sage
- Pesto Pasta with Cherry Tomatoes
- Honey Glazed Carrots
- Roasted Beet and Goat Cheese Salad
- Ratatouille with Fresh Herbs
- Balsamic Glazed Brussels Sprouts
- Herbed Chicken and Vegetable Skewers
- Tomato Basil Bruschetta
- Sweet Potato and Kale Hash
- Grilled Corn Salad with Avocado
- Cauliflower Steaks with Chimichurri Sauce
- Blueberry and Almond Pancakes
- Garlic Rosemary Roasted Potatoes
- Cucumber and Dill Greek Salad
- Rustic Tomato Tart
- Green Bean Almondine
- Pumpkin Sage Risotto
- Mixed Berry Crisp
- Lemon Garlic Asparagus
- Caprese Stuffed Portobello Mushrooms
- Watermelon Mint Salad
- Cilantro Lime Grilled Shrimp
- Creamy Broccoli and Cheddar Soup
- Roasted Red Pepper and Walnut Pesto Pasta
- Herb Marinated Grilled Chicken
- Strawberry Basil Bruschetta
- Roasted Garlic and Rosemary Focaccia
- Maple Glazed Acorn Squash
- Quinoa and Black Bean Stuffed Peppers

- Fresh Herb Omelette
- Zucchini Noodles with Pesto
- Apple Cider Glazed Pork Chops
- Roasted Tomato and Garlic Quiche
- Grilled Eggplant with Tahini Dressing
- Cranberry Walnut Quinoa Salad
- Garlic Parmesan Roasted Broccoli
- Buttermilk Herb Roasted Chicken
- Avocado and Tomato Salsa
- Ratatouille Stuffed Bell Peppers
- Lemon Thyme Grilled Salmon
- Roasted Brussels Sprouts with Cranberries
- Spaghetti Squash with Sage Brown Butter
- Grilled Peach and Arugula Salad
- Mushroom and Thyme Risotto

Roasted Vegetable Frittata

Ingredients:

- 8 large eggs
- 1/2 cup milk
- 1 cup cherry tomatoes, halved
- 1 bell pepper, diced
- 1 zucchini, sliced
- 1 red onion, thinly sliced
- 1 cup baby spinach leaves
- 1/2 cup feta cheese, crumbled
- 2 tablespoons olive oil
- 1 teaspoon dried oregano
- Salt and pepper to taste
- Fresh parsley, chopped (for garnish)

Instructions:

Preheat the oven to 375°F (190°C).

In a large bowl, whisk together the eggs and milk. Season with salt, pepper, and dried oregano. Set aside.

Heat olive oil in an oven-safe skillet over medium heat. Add the red onion and bell pepper, sautéing until softened.

Add the zucchini slices and cherry tomatoes to the skillet. Cook for an additional 2-3 minutes until the vegetables are slightly tender.

Stir in the baby spinach until it wilts.

Pour the egg mixture over the vegetables in the skillet, making sure it spreads evenly.

Sprinkle crumbled feta cheese over the top.

Transfer the skillet to the preheated oven and bake for 20-25 minutes or until the frittata is set and slightly golden on top.

Once cooked, remove from the oven and let it cool for a few minutes.

Garnish with fresh parsley and slice into wedges. Serve warm, and enjoy your delicious roasted vegetable frittata!

Spinach and Kale Salad with Fresh Berries

Ingredients:

For the Salad:

- 3 cups fresh spinach leaves, washed and dried
- 2 cups kale, stems removed and chopped
- 1 cup strawberries, hulled and sliced
- 1/2 cup blueberries
- 1/2 cup raspberries
- 1/4 cup sliced almonds, toasted
- 1/4 cup crumbled feta cheese (optional)

For the Dressing:

- 3 tablespoons extra virgin olive oil
- 2 tablespoons balsamic vinegar
- 1 tablespoon honey
- 1 teaspoon Dijon mustard
- Salt and pepper to taste

Instructions:

In a large salad bowl, combine the fresh spinach and chopped kale.
Add the sliced strawberries, blueberries, and raspberries on top.
In a dry skillet over medium heat, toast the sliced almonds until they turn golden brown. Keep a close eye on them to prevent burning.
Sprinkle the toasted almonds over the salad.
If using, crumble feta cheese on top for an added creamy texture.
In a small bowl or jar, whisk together the olive oil, balsamic vinegar, honey, Dijon mustard, salt, and pepper. Adjust the sweetness and acidity to your liking.
Drizzle the dressing over the salad just before serving.
Toss the salad gently to coat the ingredients evenly with the dressing.
Serve immediately as a refreshing and nutritious side dish or add grilled chicken or salmon for a complete meal.
Enjoy this vibrant Spinach and Kale Salad with Fresh Berries, perfect for a light and flavorful meal!

Grilled Zucchini and Tomato Skewers

Ingredients:

- 2 medium zucchinis, sliced into rounds
- 1 pint cherry tomatoes
- 2 tablespoons olive oil
- 2 cloves garlic, minced
- 1 teaspoon dried oregano
- 1 teaspoon dried basil
- Salt and pepper to taste
- Wooden or metal skewers

Instructions:

Preheat the grill to medium-high heat.
If using wooden skewers, soak them in water for at least 30 minutes to prevent burning.
In a small bowl, mix together the olive oil, minced garlic, dried oregano, dried basil, salt, and pepper to create the marinade.
Thread the zucchini rounds and cherry tomatoes onto the skewers, alternating between the two.
Brush the skewers generously with the prepared marinade, making sure to coat the vegetables evenly.
Place the skewers on the preheated grill and cook for about 8-10 minutes, turning occasionally, until the vegetables are tender and have grill marks.
During grilling, baste the skewers with any remaining marinade to enhance the flavor.
Once the zucchini and tomatoes are grilled to perfection, remove the skewers from the grill.
Serve the Grilled Zucchini and Tomato Skewers as a tasty side dish or a light appetizer.
Enjoy the smoky, savory goodness of these skewers with the combination of perfectly grilled zucchini and burst-in-your-mouth cherry tomatoes!

Lemon Herb Roast Chicken

Ingredients:

- 1 whole roasting chicken (about 4-5 pounds)
- 2 lemons, one sliced and one juiced
- 4 cloves garlic, minced
- 2 tablespoons fresh rosemary, chopped
- 2 tablespoons fresh thyme, chopped
- 1/4 cup fresh parsley, chopped
- 1/4 cup olive oil
- Salt and pepper to taste
- 1 cup chicken broth

Instructions:

Preheat the oven to 375°F (190°C).
Rinse the chicken inside and out, then pat it dry with paper towels.
In a small bowl, mix together the minced garlic, chopped rosemary, thyme, parsley, olive oil, and the juice of one lemon.
Season the chicken cavity with salt and pepper, then stuff it with the lemon slices.
Carefully lift the skin of the chicken and rub the herb mixture underneath, covering the breast and thighs.
Tie the chicken legs together with kitchen twine and tuck the wings underneath.
Place the seasoned chicken on a roasting rack in a roasting pan.
Pour the chicken broth into the bottom of the roasting pan to keep the chicken moist during cooking.
Roast the chicken in the preheated oven for approximately 1.5 to 2 hours or until the internal temperature reaches 165°F (74°C).
Baste the chicken with pan juices every 30 minutes to ensure a flavorful and moist roast.
Once done, let the chicken rest for about 10-15 minutes before carving.
Serve the Lemon Herb Roast Chicken with the pan juices and enjoy the tender, flavorful meat infused with citrus and aromatic herbs.

Quinoa-Stuffed Bell Peppers

Ingredients:

- 4 large bell peppers, halved and seeds removed
- 1 cup quinoa, rinsed
- 2 cups vegetable broth or water
- 1 tablespoon olive oil
- 1 onion, finely chopped
- 2 cloves garlic, minced
- 1 zucchini, diced
- 1 carrot, grated
- 1 cup cherry tomatoes, halved
- 1 teaspoon ground cumin
- 1 teaspoon paprika
- Salt and pepper to taste
- 1 cup black beans, cooked
- 1 cup corn kernels (fresh or frozen)
- 1/2 cup fresh cilantro, chopped
- 1 cup shredded cheese (cheddar or Mexican blend), optional
- Salsa and sour cream for serving, optional

Instructions:

Preheat the oven to 375°F (190°C).
In a medium saucepan, combine the quinoa and vegetable broth. Bring to a boil, then reduce the heat to low, cover, and simmer for 15-20 minutes, or until the quinoa is cooked and the liquid is absorbed.
While the quinoa is cooking, heat olive oil in a large skillet over medium heat. Add chopped onion and garlic, sautéing until softened.
Add diced zucchini, grated carrot, and halved cherry tomatoes to the skillet. Cook for an additional 5-7 minutes until the vegetables are tender.
Stir in ground cumin, paprika, salt, and pepper. Mix well.
In a large mixing bowl, combine the cooked quinoa, sautéed vegetables, black beans, corn, and chopped cilantro. Mix thoroughly.
Place the bell pepper halves in a baking dish. Fill each pepper half with the quinoa mixture.
If using, sprinkle shredded cheese on top of each stuffed pepper.

Cover the baking dish with foil and bake in the preheated oven for 25-30 minutes, or until the peppers are tender.

Remove the foil during the last 5 minutes of baking to allow the cheese to melt and slightly brown.

Once done, serve the Quinoa-Stuffed Bell Peppers with salsa and sour cream if desired.

Enjoy this nutritious and flavorful vegetarian dish!

Garlic and Herb Mashed Potatoes

Ingredients:

- 2 pounds (about 1 kg) potatoes, peeled and cut into chunks
- 4 cloves garlic, minced
- 1/2 cup unsalted butter
- 1 cup whole milk
- Salt and pepper to taste
- 2 tablespoons fresh chives, chopped
- 1 tablespoon fresh parsley, chopped
- 1 teaspoon fresh thyme leaves

Instructions:

Place the potato chunks in a large pot and cover them with cold water. Add a generous pinch of salt to the water.
Bring the water to a boil, then reduce the heat to simmer. Cook the potatoes until fork-tender, about 15-20 minutes.
While the potatoes are cooking, melt the butter in a small saucepan over medium heat. Add the minced garlic and sauté for 1-2 minutes until fragrant. Be careful not to let the garlic brown.
Drain the cooked potatoes and return them to the pot.
Pour the garlic-infused butter over the potatoes.
Using a potato masher or a hand mixer, mash the potatoes until smooth and creamy.
Gradually add the milk, continuing to mash until the desired consistency is reached. Add more milk if needed.
Season the mashed potatoes with salt and pepper to taste.
Stir in the chopped chives, parsley, and thyme, ensuring even distribution of herbs throughout the mashed potatoes.
Taste and adjust the seasoning if necessary.
Transfer the Garlic and Herb Mashed Potatoes to a serving bowl.
Garnish with additional fresh herbs, if desired.
Serve the mashed potatoes hot as a comforting and flavorful side dish. Enjoy!

Butternut Squash Soup with Sage

Ingredients:

- 1 medium-sized butternut squash, peeled, seeded, and diced
- 1 large onion, chopped
- 2 carrots, peeled and chopped
- 2 cloves garlic, minced
- 4 cups vegetable broth
- 1 teaspoon ground cinnamon
- 1/2 teaspoon ground nutmeg
- Salt and pepper to taste
- 2 tablespoons olive oil
- 1/4 cup fresh sage leaves, chopped (plus extra for garnish)
- 1 cup coconut milk or heavy cream (optional for added creaminess)

Instructions:

In a large pot, heat the olive oil over medium heat. Add the chopped onion, carrots, and garlic. Sauté for 5-7 minutes until the vegetables are softened.
Add the diced butternut squash to the pot and continue to cook for another 5 minutes.
Pour in the vegetable broth, ground cinnamon, ground nutmeg, salt, and pepper. Stir well to combine.
Bring the mixture to a boil, then reduce the heat to simmer. Cover the pot and let it cook for about 20-25 minutes, or until the butternut squash is tender.
While the soup is simmering, heat a small skillet over medium heat. Add the chopped sage leaves and cook for 1-2 minutes until they become fragrant and slightly crispy. Set aside for garnish.
Once the butternut squash is cooked, use an immersion blender or transfer the soup to a blender to puree until smooth.
If using, stir in the coconut milk or heavy cream for added creaminess.
Adjust the seasoning if needed.
Ladle the Butternut Squash Soup into bowls and garnish with the crispy sage leaves.
Serve hot and enjoy the comforting warmth and rich flavors of this Butternut Squash Soup with Sage.

Pesto Pasta with Cherry Tomatoes

Ingredients:

- 8 ounces (about 225g) of your favorite pasta (such as linguine or penne)
- 1 cup fresh basil leaves, packed
- 1/2 cup grated Parmesan cheese
- 1/4 cup pine nuts
- 2 cloves garlic, peeled
- 1/2 cup extra-virgin olive oil
- Salt and black pepper to taste
- 1 cup cherry tomatoes, halved
- Grated Parmesan cheese for serving
- Fresh basil leaves for garnish

Instructions:

Cook the pasta according to the package instructions in a large pot of salted boiling water. Drain and set aside.

In a food processor, combine the fresh basil, grated Parmesan cheese, pine nuts, and garlic. Pulse until coarsely chopped.

With the food processor running, slowly drizzle in the olive oil until the mixture forms a smooth and creamy pesto. Season with salt and pepper to taste.

In a large mixing bowl, toss the cooked pasta with the freshly made pesto until well coated.

Gently fold in the halved cherry tomatoes.

Taste and adjust the seasoning if necessary.

Serve the Pesto Pasta with Cherry Tomatoes hot or at room temperature.

Garnish with additional grated Parmesan cheese and fresh basil leaves.

Enjoy this simple and delicious pasta dish that celebrates the vibrant flavors of basil and tomatoes!

Honey Glazed Carrots

Ingredients:

- 1 pound (about 450g) carrots, peeled and sliced into coins or sticks
- 2 tablespoons unsalted butter
- 2 tablespoons honey
- 1 tablespoon fresh parsley, chopped (for garnish)
- Salt and pepper to taste

Instructions:

In a medium-sized saucepan, bring water to a boil. Add a pinch of salt.
Add the sliced carrots to the boiling water and cook for about 5-7 minutes or until they are just tender. Drain and set aside.
In a large skillet or pan, melt the butter over medium heat.
Add the honey to the melted butter and stir until well combined.
Add the blanched carrots to the skillet, tossing them in the honey butter mixture until they are evenly coated.
Allow the carrots to cook in the honey glaze for an additional 3-5 minutes, stirring occasionally, until the carrots are tender and glazed.
Season with salt and pepper to taste. Adjust the sweetness if needed by adding more honey.
Transfer the Honey Glazed Carrots to a serving dish.
Garnish with chopped fresh parsley for a burst of color and added freshness.
Serve the honey glazed carrots as a delightful side dish alongside your main course.
Enjoy the perfect balance of sweetness and savory flavors in these Honey Glazed Carrots!

Roasted Beet and Goat Cheese Salad

Ingredients:

For the Salad:

- 4 medium-sized beets, peeled and cubed
- 4 cups mixed salad greens (arugula, spinach, or your choice)
- 1/2 cup walnuts, toasted and chopped
- 1/4 cup red onion, thinly sliced
- 4 ounces goat cheese, crumbled
- Salt and pepper to taste

For the Balsamic Vinaigrette:

- 1/4 cup balsamic vinegar
- 1/2 cup extra-virgin olive oil
- 1 tablespoon Dijon mustard
- 1 teaspoon honey
- Salt and pepper to taste

Instructions:

Preheat the oven to 400°F (200°C).

Place the cubed beets on a baking sheet. Drizzle with olive oil and season with salt and pepper. Toss to coat evenly.

Roast the beets in the preheated oven for 25-30 minutes or until they are tender when pierced with a fork. Allow them to cool slightly.

While the beets are roasting, prepare the balsamic vinaigrette. In a small bowl, whisk together balsamic vinegar, olive oil, Dijon mustard, honey, salt, and pepper until well combined.

In a large salad bowl, assemble the mixed salad greens.

Add the roasted beets, toasted walnuts, and thinly sliced red onion to the salad greens.

Drizzle the balsamic vinaigrette over the salad and toss gently to coat the ingredients.

Sprinkle crumbled goat cheese on top of the salad.

Taste and adjust the seasoning if necessary.

Serve the Roasted Beet and Goat Cheese Salad immediately, allowing the warm beets to slightly wilt the greens.

Enjoy this vibrant and flavorful salad as a refreshing appetizer or a light, wholesome meal!

Ratatouille with Fresh Herbs

Ingredients:

- 1 large eggplant, diced
- 2 medium zucchinis, sliced
- 1 large bell pepper, diced (use a mix of colors if available)
- 1 large onion, diced
- 3 cloves garlic, minced
- 4 large tomatoes, diced
- 1/4 cup tomato paste
- 1 teaspoon dried oregano
- 1 teaspoon dried thyme
- 1 teaspoon dried rosemary
- Salt and pepper to taste
- 1/4 cup fresh basil, chopped
- 1/4 cup fresh parsley, chopped
- 2 tablespoons olive oil

Instructions:

Preheat the oven to 375°F (190°C).
In a large skillet, heat the olive oil over medium heat.
Add the diced onion and minced garlic to the skillet. Sauté until the onions are translucent.
Add the diced eggplant, zucchini, and bell pepper to the skillet. Cook for about 5-7 minutes until the vegetables start to soften.
Stir in the diced tomatoes, tomato paste, dried oregano, dried thyme, dried rosemary, salt, and pepper. Mix well.
Simmer the mixture for an additional 10-12 minutes, allowing the flavors to meld.
Transfer the vegetable mixture to a baking dish.
Bake in the preheated oven for 25-30 minutes or until the vegetables are tender.
Remove the Ratatouille from the oven and stir in the fresh basil and parsley.
Taste and adjust the seasoning if necessary.
Serve the Ratatouille with Fresh Herbs as a side dish or over a bed of couscous, rice, or pasta.
Enjoy the delightful combination of flavors and the aromatic freshness of the herbs in this classic French dish!

Balsamic Glazed Brussels Sprouts

Ingredients:

- 1 pound Brussels sprouts, trimmed and halved
- 2 tablespoons olive oil
- Salt and pepper to taste
- 3 tablespoons balsamic vinegar
- 2 tablespoons honey or maple syrup
- 2 cloves garlic, minced
- 1/4 cup grated Parmesan cheese (optional)
- 2 tablespoons fresh parsley, chopped (for garnish)

Instructions:

Preheat the oven to 400°F (200°C).
In a large bowl, toss the halved Brussels sprouts with olive oil, salt, and pepper until evenly coated.
Spread the Brussels sprouts on a baking sheet in a single layer.
Roast in the preheated oven for 20-25 minutes or until the Brussels sprouts are golden brown and crisp on the edges.
While the Brussels sprouts are roasting, prepare the balsamic glaze. In a small saucepan over medium heat, combine balsamic vinegar, honey (or maple syrup), and minced garlic. Bring to a simmer, then reduce the heat and let it cook for 5-7 minutes or until the mixture has thickened slightly.
Once the Brussels sprouts are done roasting, transfer them to a serving bowl.
Drizzle the balsamic glaze over the roasted Brussels sprouts and toss gently to coat.
If desired, sprinkle grated Parmesan cheese over the Brussels sprouts and toss again.
Garnish with fresh chopped parsley.
Taste and adjust the seasoning if necessary.
Serve the Balsamic Glazed Brussels Sprouts as a delicious side dish for any meal.
Enjoy the sweet and tangy flavors of these beautifully glazed Brussels sprouts!

Herbed Chicken and Vegetable Skewers

Ingredients:

For the Marinade:

- 1.5 pounds (about 700g) boneless, skinless chicken breasts, cut into chunks
- 1/4 cup olive oil
- 2 tablespoons fresh lemon juice
- 3 cloves garlic, minced
- 1 tablespoon fresh rosemary, chopped
- 1 tablespoon fresh thyme, chopped
- 1 teaspoon dried oregano
- Salt and black pepper to taste

For the Skewers:

- 1 red bell pepper, cut into chunks
- 1 yellow bell pepper, cut into chunks
- 1 red onion, cut into chunks
- Cherry tomatoes
- Zucchini, sliced
- Wooden or metal skewers

Instructions:

If using wooden skewers, soak them in water for at least 30 minutes to prevent burning.

In a bowl, whisk together olive oil, lemon juice, minced garlic, chopped rosemary, chopped thyme, dried oregano, salt, and black pepper to create the marinade.

Place the chicken chunks in a large zip-top bag or shallow dish. Pour the marinade over the chicken, ensuring it's well coated. Marinate in the refrigerator for at least 30 minutes, or preferably a few hours.

Preheat the grill or grill pan to medium-high heat.

Thread the marinated chicken pieces, bell pepper chunks, onion chunks, cherry tomatoes, and zucchini slices onto the skewers, alternating for a colorful mix.

Brush the skewers with any remaining marinade for added flavor.

Grill the skewers for about 10-15 minutes, turning occasionally, until the chicken is cooked through and has a nice char on the edges.

While grilling, baste the skewers with any leftover marinade for extra flavor.
Once the chicken is fully cooked and the vegetables are tender, remove the skewers from the grill.
Serve the Herbed Chicken and Vegetable Skewers hot, garnished with additional fresh herbs if desired.
Enjoy these flavorful and herb-infused skewers as a delicious and wholesome meal!

Tomato Basil Bruschetta

Ingredients:

- 4-5 ripe tomatoes, diced
- 1/4 cup fresh basil, chopped
- 3 cloves garlic, minced
- 2 tablespoons extra-virgin olive oil
- 1 teaspoon balsamic vinegar
- Salt and black pepper to taste
- Baguette or Italian bread, sliced
- 1 clove garlic, peeled (for rubbing on the bread)

Instructions:

In a medium bowl, combine the diced tomatoes, chopped fresh basil, minced garlic, extra-virgin olive oil, balsamic vinegar, salt, and black pepper. Mix well to ensure all ingredients are evenly incorporated.

Let the tomato mixture sit for about 15-20 minutes to allow the flavors to meld.

Preheat your oven broiler or grill.

Slice the baguette or Italian bread into 1/2-inch thick slices.

Place the bread slices on a baking sheet and toast under the broiler or on the grill for 1-2 minutes per side, or until golden brown.

While the bread is still warm, rub each slice with a peeled clove of garlic. This adds a subtle garlic flavor to the bruschetta.

Spoon the tomato and basil mixture generously over each toasted bread slice.

Drizzle with a little extra olive oil and sprinkle with additional chopped basil for garnish.

Serve the Tomato Basil Bruschetta immediately as a delightful appetizer or snack.

Enjoy the fresh and vibrant flavors of this classic Italian dish!

Sweet Potato and Kale Hash

Ingredients:

- 2 large sweet potatoes, peeled and diced
- 1 bunch kale, stems removed and leaves chopped
- 1 red onion, finely chopped
- 2 cloves garlic, minced
- 2 tablespoons olive oil
- 1 teaspoon smoked paprika
- 1/2 teaspoon ground cumin
- Salt and pepper to taste
- Poached or fried eggs (optional, for serving)

Instructions:

Heat olive oil in a large skillet over medium heat.

Add the diced sweet potatoes to the skillet and cook for about 8-10 minutes, stirring occasionally, until they start to soften and brown.

Add the chopped red onion to the skillet and sauté for an additional 3-5 minutes until the onion becomes translucent.

Stir in the minced garlic, smoked paprika, ground cumin, salt, and pepper. Cook for another 1-2 minutes until the spices are fragrant.

Add the chopped kale to the skillet, tossing and cooking until the kale wilts and becomes tender. This should take about 3-5 minutes.

Taste and adjust the seasoning if needed.

If desired, make wells in the hash and crack the eggs into them. Cover the skillet and cook until the eggs are done to your liking.

Serve the Sweet Potato and Kale Hash hot, with poached or fried eggs on top if you've added them.

Enjoy this hearty and nutritious hash as a satisfying breakfast or brunch option!

Grilled Corn Salad with Avocado

Ingredients:

- 4 ears of corn, husked
- 1 avocado, diced
- 1 cup cherry tomatoes, halved
- 1/4 cup red onion, finely chopped
- 1/4 cup fresh cilantro, chopped
- 1 jalapeño, seeds removed and finely chopped (optional for heat)
- Juice of 2 limes
- 2 tablespoons olive oil
- Salt and pepper to taste
- Crumbled feta or cotija cheese (optional, for garnish)

Instructions:

Preheat the grill to medium-high heat.
Place the husked ears of corn on the grill and cook for 8-10 minutes, turning occasionally, until the corn is charred and cooked through. Remove from the grill and let them cool.
Once the corn is cool enough to handle, cut the kernels off the cobs into a large bowl.
Add diced avocado, halved cherry tomatoes, finely chopped red onion, chopped cilantro, and jalapeño to the bowl with the grilled corn.
In a small bowl, whisk together lime juice, olive oil, salt, and pepper to create the dressing.
Pour the dressing over the salad and gently toss to combine, ensuring the ingredients are well coated.
If desired, sprinkle crumbled feta or cotija cheese over the top.
Taste and adjust the seasoning if necessary.
Chill the Grilled Corn Salad with Avocado in the refrigerator for about 30 minutes before serving to let the flavors meld.
Serve as a refreshing side dish for grilled meats or as a standalone salad.
Enjoy the vibrant colors and flavors of this delicious summer salad!

Cauliflower Steaks with Chimichurri Sauce

Ingredients:

For Cauliflower Steaks:

- 1 large head of cauliflower
- 3 tablespoons olive oil
- 1 teaspoon smoked paprika
- 1 teaspoon garlic powder
- Salt and black pepper to taste

For Chimichurri Sauce:

- 1 cup fresh parsley, chopped
- 1/4 cup fresh cilantro, chopped
- 3 cloves garlic, minced
- 1/2 cup extra-virgin olive oil
- 3 tablespoons red wine vinegar
- 1 teaspoon dried oregano
- 1/2 teaspoon red pepper flakes (adjust to taste)
- Salt and black pepper to taste

Instructions:

Preheat the oven to 425°F (220°C).

Remove the leaves from the cauliflower and trim the stem. Cut the cauliflower into 1-inch thick slices to create "steaks."

In a small bowl, mix olive oil, smoked paprika, garlic powder, salt, and black pepper. Brush the cauliflower steaks on both sides with this mixture.

Place the cauliflower steaks on a baking sheet lined with parchment paper or a greased baking dish.

Roast the cauliflower in the preheated oven for 25-30 minutes or until the edges are golden brown and the cauliflower is tender.

While the cauliflower is roasting, prepare the chimichurri sauce. In a bowl, combine chopped parsley, chopped cilantro, minced garlic, olive oil, red wine vinegar, dried oregano, red pepper flakes, salt, and black pepper. Mix well.

Once the cauliflower steaks are done, transfer them to serving plates.

Spoon the chimichurri sauce generously over each cauliflower steak.

Serve the Cauliflower Steaks with Chimichurri Sauce as a flavorful and satisfying vegetarian main course.

Enjoy the hearty and savory goodness of this dish with the vibrant flavors of chimichurri!

Blueberry and Almond Pancakes

Ingredients:

- 1 cup all-purpose flour
- 1 tablespoon sugar
- 1 teaspoon baking powder
- 1/2 teaspoon baking soda
- 1/4 teaspoon salt
- 1 cup buttermilk
- 1 large egg
- 2 tablespoons unsalted butter, melted
- 1 teaspoon almond extract
- 1/2 cup blueberries (fresh or frozen)
- 1/4 cup sliced almonds
- Maple syrup and additional blueberries for serving

Instructions:

In a large mixing bowl, whisk together the flour, sugar, baking powder, baking soda, and salt.

In a separate bowl, beat the egg and then add the buttermilk, melted butter, and almond extract. Mix well.

Pour the wet ingredients into the dry ingredients and stir until just combined. Be careful not to overmix; a few lumps are okay.

Gently fold in the blueberries and sliced almonds into the batter.

Heat a griddle or non-stick skillet over medium heat. Lightly grease with butter or cooking spray.

Pour 1/4 cup portions of batter onto the griddle for each pancake.

Cook until bubbles form on the surface of the pancake, then flip and cook the other side until golden brown.

Repeat until all the batter is used, adjusting the heat if necessary.

Serve the Blueberry and Almond Pancakes hot, topped with additional blueberries, sliced almonds, and a drizzle of maple syrup.

Enjoy a delicious and delightful breakfast with the perfect combination of sweet blueberries and nutty almonds!

Garlic Rosemary Roasted Potatoes

Ingredients:

- 2 pounds (about 1 kg) baby potatoes, washed and halved
- 3 tablespoons olive oil
- 4 cloves garlic, minced
- 1 tablespoon fresh rosemary, finely chopped
- Salt and black pepper to taste
- 1 tablespoon grated Parmesan cheese (optional, for garnish)
- Fresh parsley, chopped (for garnish)

Instructions:

Preheat the oven to 425°F (220°C).
In a large bowl, combine the halved baby potatoes, olive oil, minced garlic, chopped rosemary, salt, and black pepper. Toss until the potatoes are evenly coated with the seasonings.
Spread the potatoes in a single layer on a baking sheet lined with parchment paper or greased with cooking spray.
Roast the potatoes in the preheated oven for 30-35 minutes or until they are golden brown and crispy on the edges. Stir halfway through the cooking time for even roasting.
Once the potatoes are done, remove them from the oven.
If desired, sprinkle grated Parmesan cheese over the hot roasted potatoes and toss to melt the cheese.
Transfer the Garlic Rosemary Roasted Potatoes to a serving dish.
Garnish with chopped fresh parsley for a burst of color and added freshness.
Serve the roasted potatoes as a flavorful side dish to accompany your favorite main course.
Enjoy the crispy exteriors and tender interiors of these Garlic Rosemary Roasted Potatoes with the aromatic blend of garlic and rosemary!

Cucumber and Dill Greek Salad

Ingredients:

For the Salad:

- 2 cucumbers, diced
- 2 cups cherry tomatoes, halved
- 1 cup Kalamata olives, pitted
- 1 cup feta cheese, crumbled
- 1/2 red onion, thinly sliced
- 1/4 cup fresh dill, chopped
- Salt and black pepper to taste

For the Dressing:

- 1/4 cup extra-virgin olive oil
- 2 tablespoons red wine vinegar
- 1 teaspoon Dijon mustard
- 1 clove garlic, minced
- 1 teaspoon dried oregano
- Salt and black pepper to taste

Instructions:

In a large salad bowl, combine diced cucumbers, halved cherry tomatoes, Kalamata olives, crumbled feta cheese, thinly sliced red onion, and chopped fresh dill.

In a separate small bowl, whisk together extra-virgin olive oil, red wine vinegar, Dijon mustard, minced garlic, dried oregano, salt, and black pepper to create the dressing.

Pour the dressing over the salad and toss gently to ensure all ingredients are well coated.

Taste and adjust the seasoning if necessary.

Chill the Cucumber and Dill Greek Salad in the refrigerator for at least 30 minutes before serving to let the flavors meld.

Serve as a refreshing and tangy side dish alongside grilled meats, fish, or as a standalone light meal.

Enjoy the crispness of cucumbers, the burst of cherry tomatoes, the brininess of olives, and the herby freshness of dill in this delightful Greek-inspired salad!

Rustic Tomato Tart

Ingredients:

For the Tart Crust:

- 1 1/4 cups all-purpose flour
- 1/2 cup unsalted butter, cold and cubed
- 1/4 teaspoon salt
- 3-4 tablespoons ice water

For the Filling:

- 4-5 large tomatoes, sliced
- 1 cup mozzarella cheese, shredded
- 1/2 cup Parmesan cheese, grated
- 2 tablespoons Dijon mustard
- 2 cloves garlic, minced
- 2 tablespoons fresh basil, chopped
- Salt and black pepper to taste

For the Glaze:

- 1 tablespoon balsamic glaze (optional)
- Fresh basil leaves for garnish

Instructions:

Tart Crust:

In a food processor, combine the flour, cold cubed butter, and salt. Pulse until the mixture resembles coarse crumbs.
Add ice water, one tablespoon at a time, and pulse until the dough comes together.
Turn the dough out onto a floured surface, knead it into a disc, wrap it in plastic wrap, and refrigerate for at least 30 minutes.

Filling:

Preheat the oven to 400°F (200°C).
Roll out the chilled dough on a floured surface into a rustic circle, about 12 inches in diameter.
Transfer the rolled-out dough to a baking sheet lined with parchment paper.
Spread Dijon mustard over the surface of the dough, leaving a border around the edges.
Sprinkle half of the shredded mozzarella and Parmesan cheese over the mustard.
Arrange the sliced tomatoes on top of the cheese.
In a small bowl, mix together minced garlic and the remaining cheese. Sprinkle this mixture over the tomatoes.
Season the tart with salt and black pepper, then fold the edges of the dough over the filling, creating a rustic border.
Bake in the preheated oven for 25-30 minutes or until the crust is golden brown.

Glaze and Garnish:

Once out of the oven, drizzle the balsamic glaze over the top of the tart.
Garnish with fresh chopped basil leaves.
Let the Rustic Tomato Tart cool slightly before slicing.
Serve warm or at room temperature, and enjoy this delightful combination of flaky crust, juicy tomatoes, and melted cheese!

Green Bean Almondine

Ingredients:

- 1 pound (about 450g) fresh green beans, ends trimmed
- 2 tablespoons olive oil
- 1/2 cup sliced almonds
- 2 cloves garlic, minced
- Zest of 1 lemon
- 2 tablespoons fresh lemon juice
- Salt and black pepper to taste
- Chopped fresh parsley for garnish

Instructions:

Bring a large pot of salted water to a boil. Add the green beans and cook for 3-5 minutes or until they are crisp-tender. Drain and immediately transfer the beans to an ice water bath to stop the cooking process. Drain again and set aside.
In a large skillet, heat olive oil over medium heat.
Add sliced almonds to the skillet and toast them for 2-3 minutes until they are golden brown, stirring occasionally.
Add minced garlic to the skillet and sauté for 1-2 minutes until fragrant.
Add the blanched green beans to the skillet, tossing to coat them with the almond and garlic mixture.
Pour in the fresh lemon juice and sprinkle lemon zest over the green beans. Continue to toss until the beans are heated through.
Season with salt and black pepper to taste. Adjust the seasoning if necessary.
Transfer the Green Bean Almondine to a serving dish.
Garnish with chopped fresh parsley for a burst of color and added freshness.
Serve immediately as a delightful side dish that showcases the vibrant flavors of green beans and almonds.
Enjoy the crisp-tender green beans with the crunch of toasted almonds in this classic and elegant dish!

Pumpkin Sage Risotto

Ingredients:

- 1 cup Arborio rice
- 1/2 cup dry white wine
- 4 cups vegetable or chicken broth, kept warm
- 1 cup canned pumpkin puree
- 1 small onion, finely chopped
- 2 cloves garlic, minced
- 1/2 cup Parmesan cheese, grated
- 2 tablespoons fresh sage, chopped
- 2 tablespoons unsalted butter
- 2 tablespoons olive oil
- Salt and black pepper to taste

Instructions:

In a medium-sized saucepan, heat the vegetable or chicken broth over low heat to keep it warm.

In a large skillet or wide saucepan, heat olive oil over medium heat. Add chopped onion and sauté until it becomes translucent.

Add minced garlic to the skillet and sauté for an additional 1-2 minutes until fragrant.

Stir in Arborio rice and cook for 1-2 minutes, allowing the rice to toast slightly.

Pour in the white wine, stirring constantly until most of the liquid is absorbed.

Begin adding the warm broth, one ladle at a time, stirring frequently. Wait until the liquid is almost fully absorbed before adding the next ladle of broth.

Continue this process until the rice is creamy and cooked to al dente, which usually takes about 18-20 minutes.

Stir in the canned pumpkin puree and chopped sage, incorporating it well into the risotto.

Once the pumpkin is well combined, stir in grated Parmesan cheese, butter, salt, and black pepper. Mix until the cheese and butter are melted, and the risotto is creamy.

Taste and adjust the seasoning if necessary.

Serve the Pumpkin Sage Risotto hot, garnished with additional fresh sage and a sprinkle of Parmesan cheese.

Enjoy this rich and flavorful autumn-inspired dish!

Mixed Berry Crisp

Ingredients:

For the Berry Filling:

- 3 cups mixed berries (strawberries, blueberries, raspberries, blackberries)
- 1/4 cup granulated sugar
- 2 tablespoons cornstarch
- 1 tablespoon fresh lemon juice
- Zest of 1 lemon

For the Crisp Topping:

- 1 cup old-fashioned rolled oats
- 1/2 cup all-purpose flour
- 1/2 cup brown sugar, packed
- 1/4 teaspoon salt
- 1/2 cup unsalted butter, cold and diced
- Vanilla ice cream or whipped cream for serving (optional)

Instructions:

Preheat the oven to 350°F (175°C).
In a large bowl, combine the mixed berries, granulated sugar, cornstarch, fresh lemon juice, and lemon zest. Toss until the berries are well coated.
Transfer the berry mixture to a baking dish, spreading it out evenly.
In another bowl, mix together the rolled oats, all-purpose flour, brown sugar, and salt for the crisp topping.
Add the cold, diced butter to the dry mixture. Use your fingers or a pastry cutter to incorporate the butter until the mixture resembles coarse crumbs.
Sprinkle the crisp topping evenly over the berries in the baking dish.
Bake in the preheated oven for 30-35 minutes or until the topping is golden brown, and the berries are bubbly.
Remove from the oven and let it cool slightly before serving.
Serve the Mixed Berry Crisp warm, optionally topped with vanilla ice cream or whipped cream.
Enjoy this delightful and comforting dessert that highlights the sweet and tart flavors of mixed berries!

Lemon Garlic Asparagus

Ingredients:

- 1 pound (about 450g) fresh asparagus, trimmed
- 2 tablespoons olive oil
- 2 cloves garlic, minced
- Zest of 1 lemon
- Juice of 1 lemon
- Salt and black pepper to taste
- Grated Parmesan cheese for garnish (optional)

Instructions:

Preheat the oven to 400°F (200°C).
In a large bowl, toss the trimmed asparagus with olive oil, minced garlic, lemon zest, lemon juice, salt, and black pepper. Make sure the asparagus is evenly coated.
Spread the asparagus in a single layer on a baking sheet lined with parchment paper.
Roast in the preheated oven for 12-15 minutes, or until the asparagus is tender but still crisp.
If desired, sprinkle grated Parmesan cheese over the roasted asparagus during the last 5 minutes of cooking for added flavor.
Remove from the oven and transfer the Lemon Garlic Asparagus to a serving dish.
Garnish with additional lemon zest and a squeeze of fresh lemon juice.
Serve hot as a vibrant and flavorful side dish for your favorite main course.
Enjoy the zesty combination of lemon and garlic that enhances the natural freshness of asparagus!

Caprese Stuffed Portobello Mushrooms

Ingredients:

- 4 large Portobello mushrooms, stems removed
- 2 tablespoons olive oil
- 4 medium-sized tomatoes, sliced
- 1 ball fresh mozzarella cheese, sliced
- Fresh basil leaves
- Balsamic glaze, for drizzling
- Salt and black pepper to taste

Instructions:

Preheat the oven to 400°F (200°C).
Clean the Portobello mushrooms and remove the stems. Place them on a baking sheet.
Drizzle olive oil over the mushrooms and season with salt and black pepper.
Arrange tomato slices, fresh mozzarella slices, and fresh basil leaves inside each Portobello mushroom.
Bake in the preheated oven for 15-20 minutes or until the mushrooms are tender and the cheese is melted.
Remove from the oven and drizzle balsamic glaze over the stuffed mushrooms.
Serve the Caprese Stuffed Portobello Mushrooms hot, garnished with additional fresh basil if desired.
Enjoy this delicious and satisfying dish that brings together the classic Caprese flavors in a delightful mushroom vessel!

Watermelon Mint Salad

Ingredients:

- 4 cups seedless watermelon, cubed
- 1 cucumber, peeled and diced
- 1/2 cup feta cheese, crumbled
- 1/4 cup fresh mint leaves, chopped
- 1 tablespoon extra-virgin olive oil
- 1 tablespoon balsamic glaze
- Salt and black pepper to taste

Instructions:

In a large bowl, combine the cubed watermelon and diced cucumber.
Add crumbled feta cheese and chopped fresh mint leaves to the bowl.
Drizzle extra-virgin olive oil over the salad.
Gently toss the ingredients to combine, ensuring even distribution of flavors.
Drizzle balsamic glaze over the salad for a touch of sweetness and tanginess.
Season with salt and black pepper to taste.
Toss the Watermelon Mint Salad one more time before serving.
Chill in the refrigerator for about 30 minutes before serving for a refreshing experience.
Serve the salad in individual bowls or on a platter.
Enjoy the sweet, savory, and minty flavors that make this Watermelon Mint Salad a perfect summer delight!

Cilantro Lime Grilled Shrimp

Ingredients:

- 1 pound large shrimp, peeled and deveined
- 3 tablespoons olive oil
- 3 cloves garlic, minced
- 1/4 cup fresh cilantro, chopped
- Zest and juice of 2 limes
- 1 teaspoon cumin
- 1 teaspoon paprika
- Salt and black pepper to taste
- Lime wedges for serving

Instructions:

In a bowl, whisk together olive oil, minced garlic, chopped cilantro, lime zest, lime juice, cumin, paprika, salt, and black pepper to create the marinade.
Add the peeled and deveined shrimp to the marinade, ensuring they are well coated. Allow them to marinate for at least 15-30 minutes in the refrigerator.
Preheat the grill to medium-high heat.
Thread the marinated shrimp onto skewers, ensuring they are evenly spaced.
Grill the shrimp for 2-3 minutes per side or until they are opaque and have nice grill marks.
While grilling, baste the shrimp with any remaining marinade for added flavor.
Once the shrimp are done, remove them from the grill.
Serve the Cilantro Lime Grilled Shrimp hot, garnished with additional chopped cilantro and lime wedges on the side.
Enjoy these succulent and flavorful grilled shrimp as a tasty appetizer or as part of a delicious main course!

Creamy Broccoli and Cheddar Soup

Ingredients:

- 4 cups broccoli florets
- 1 onion, chopped
- 2 carrots, peeled and chopped
- 3 cups vegetable or chicken broth
- 2 cups sharp cheddar cheese, shredded
- 2 cups whole milk
- 1/4 cup all-purpose flour
- 3 tablespoons unsalted butter
- 2 cloves garlic, minced
- 1/4 teaspoon nutmeg
- Salt and black pepper to taste

Instructions:

In a large pot, melt the butter over medium heat. Add chopped onion and carrots. Sauté for 3-4 minutes until the vegetables begin to soften.

Add minced garlic to the pot and sauté for an additional 1-2 minutes until fragrant.

Sprinkle flour over the vegetables and stir to create a roux. Cook for 2-3 minutes to eliminate the raw flour taste.

Gradually whisk in the vegetable or chicken broth, ensuring there are no lumps. Bring the mixture to a simmer.

Add broccoli florets to the pot and simmer for about 10-12 minutes, or until the broccoli is tender.

Using an immersion blender or transferring to a blender in batches, blend the soup until smooth.

Return the blended soup to the pot over low heat. Stir in whole milk and shredded cheddar cheese until the cheese is melted and the soup is creamy.

Season with nutmeg, salt, and black pepper. Adjust the seasoning to taste.

Simmer for an additional 5-7 minutes, allowing the flavors to meld.

Serve the Creamy Broccoli and Cheddar Soup hot, optionally garnished with additional shredded cheddar or a sprinkle of nutmeg.

Enjoy this comforting and cheesy soup as a delicious appetizer or a hearty main course!

Roasted Red Pepper and Walnut Pesto Pasta

Ingredients:

For the Pesto:

- 2 large red bell peppers, roasted and peeled
- 1/2 cup walnuts, toasted
- 2 cloves garlic, minced
- 1/2 cup Parmesan cheese, grated
- 1/2 cup fresh basil leaves
- 1/2 cup extra-virgin olive oil
- Salt and black pepper to taste

For the Pasta:

- 12 ounces (340g) pasta of your choice
- Salt for boiling water
- Extra Parmesan cheese and fresh basil for garnish

Instructions:

Roasting Red Peppers:

Preheat the oven to broil.
Place the red peppers on a baking sheet and broil, turning occasionally, until the skin is charred and blistered.
Transfer the roasted peppers to a bowl, cover with plastic wrap, and let them steam for about 10 minutes.
Peel off the charred skin, remove the seeds, and set aside.

To Make the Pesto:

In a food processor, combine the roasted red peppers, toasted walnuts, minced garlic, grated Parmesan cheese, and fresh basil leaves.
Pulse the ingredients until coarsely chopped.

With the processor running, slowly drizzle in the olive oil until the pesto reaches your desired consistency.
Season with salt and black pepper to taste. Set aside.

For the Pasta:

Cook the pasta in a large pot of salted boiling water according to the package instructions until al dente.
Reserve a cup of pasta cooking water and then drain the pasta.

Assembling:

In a large bowl, toss the cooked pasta with the roasted red pepper and walnut pesto. If needed, add a bit of the reserved pasta cooking water to loosen the sauce.
Garnish with extra grated Parmesan cheese and fresh basil leaves.
Serve the Roasted Red Pepper and Walnut Pesto Pasta immediately.

Enjoy this vibrant and flavorful pasta dish with the goodness of roasted red peppers and crunchy walnuts!

Herb Marinated Grilled Chicken

Ingredients:

- 4 boneless, skinless chicken breasts
- 1/4 cup olive oil
- 3 tablespoons fresh lemon juice
- 2 cloves garlic, minced
- 1 tablespoon fresh rosemary, chopped
- 1 tablespoon fresh thyme, chopped
- 1 tablespoon fresh parsley, chopped
- Salt and black pepper to taste
- Lemon wedges for serving

Instructions:

In a bowl, whisk together olive oil, fresh lemon juice, minced garlic, chopped rosemary, chopped thyme, chopped parsley, salt, and black pepper to create the marinade.
Place the chicken breasts in a large resealable plastic bag or shallow dish.
Pour the marinade over the chicken, ensuring that it is well coated. Seal the bag or cover the dish, and marinate in the refrigerator for at least 30 minutes. For more flavor, you can marinate for several hours or overnight.
Preheat the grill to medium-high heat.
Remove the chicken from the marinade and let any excess drip off.
Grill the chicken for approximately 6-8 minutes per side or until the internal temperature reaches 165°F (74°C) and the chicken is fully cooked.
While grilling, baste the chicken with any remaining marinade for added flavor.
Once the chicken is done, remove it from the grill and let it rest for a few minutes.
Serve the Herb Marinated Grilled Chicken hot, garnished with additional fresh herbs and lemon wedges on the side.
Enjoy these juicy and flavorful grilled chicken breasts as a delicious and wholesome main course!

Strawberry Basil Bruschetta

Ingredients:

- 1 French baguette, sliced into 1/2-inch thick rounds
- 1 cup strawberries, diced
- 1/4 cup fresh basil, chopped
- 1 tablespoon balsamic glaze
- 1 tablespoon honey
- 4 ounces goat cheese, softened
- Olive oil for drizzling
- Salt and black pepper to taste

Instructions:

Preheat your oven broiler or grill.
Arrange the baguette slices on a baking sheet.
Drizzle olive oil over the bread slices and place them under the broiler or on the grill for 1-2 minutes per side, or until golden brown.
In a bowl, combine diced strawberries and chopped fresh basil. Mix gently.
Drizzle balsamic glaze and honey over the strawberry and basil mixture. Add salt and black pepper to taste. Toss to combine.
Spread a generous amount of softened goat cheese on each toasted baguette slice.
Spoon the strawberry and basil mixture over the goat cheese-topped baguette slices.
Drizzle a little extra balsamic glaze over the top for additional flavor.
Serve the Strawberry Basil Bruschetta immediately as a refreshing and delightful appetizer.
Enjoy the sweet and savory combination of strawberries, basil, and goat cheese on crispy baguette slices!

Roasted Garlic and Rosemary Focaccia

Ingredients:

For the Focaccia Dough:

- 4 cups all-purpose flour
- 1 1/2 cups warm water
- 2 teaspoons active dry yeast
- 1 teaspoon sugar
- 1/4 cup olive oil
- 1 teaspoon salt

For the Topping:

- 1/4 cup olive oil
- 1 head of garlic, roasted
- Fresh rosemary leaves
- Coarse sea salt

Instructions:

For the Focaccia Dough:

In a small bowl, combine warm water, active dry yeast, and sugar. Let it sit for 5-10 minutes until frothy.
In a large mixing bowl, combine the flour and salt. Make a well in the center.
Pour the yeast mixture and olive oil into the well. Stir with a wooden spoon until a dough forms.
Turn the dough onto a floured surface and knead for about 8-10 minutes until it becomes smooth and elastic.
Place the dough in a lightly oiled bowl, cover with a clean kitchen towel, and let it rise in a warm place for 1-2 hours or until it doubles in size.

For the Topping:

Preheat the oven to 425°F (220°C).
Cut off the top of the head of garlic to expose the cloves. Drizzle with olive oil, wrap in foil, and roast in the oven for about 30-40 minutes, or until the cloves are soft and golden.

Assembling the Focaccia:

Punch down the risen dough and transfer it to a greased baking sheet. Press it out to cover the pan evenly.
Drizzle olive oil over the top of the dough, making sure it gets into the dimples.
Squeeze the roasted garlic cloves from the head and distribute them evenly on the dough.
Sprinkle fresh rosemary leaves over the top and generously season with coarse sea salt.
Allow the dough to rise again for about 20-30 minutes.
Bake in the preheated oven for 20-25 minutes or until the focaccia is golden brown and sounds hollow when tapped.
Remove from the oven and let it cool slightly before slicing.
Serve the Roasted Garlic and Rosemary Focaccia warm as an appetizer or side dish.
Enjoy the aromatic blend of roasted garlic and rosemary in this soft and flavorful focaccia!

Maple Glazed Acorn Squash

Ingredients:

- 2 acorn squash, halved and seeds removed
- 1/4 cup melted butter
- 1/4 cup maple syrup
- 2 tablespoons brown sugar
- 1 teaspoon ground cinnamon
- 1/2 teaspoon ground nutmeg
- Salt to taste
- Chopped fresh parsley or thyme for garnish (optional)

Instructions:

Preheat the oven to 400°F (200°C).
Place the acorn squash halves, cut side up, on a baking sheet.
In a small bowl, mix together melted butter, maple syrup, brown sugar, ground cinnamon, ground nutmeg, and a pinch of salt.
Brush the maple glaze generously over the cut surfaces and edges of the acorn squash.
Roast in the preheated oven for 35-45 minutes or until the squash is tender and caramelized around the edges.
Baste the squash with the maple glaze from the pan halfway through the cooking time.
Remove from the oven and let it cool for a few minutes.
Optional: Garnish with chopped fresh parsley or thyme for a burst of freshness.
Serve the Maple Glazed Acorn Squash halves warm as a delightful side dish.
Enjoy the sweet and savory flavors of this deliciously glazed acorn squash!

Quinoa and Black Bean Stuffed Peppers

Ingredients:

- 4 large bell peppers, halved and seeds removed
- 1 cup quinoa, cooked according to package instructions
- 1 can (15 ounces) black beans, drained and rinsed
- 1 cup corn kernels (fresh, frozen, or canned)
- 1 cup cherry tomatoes, diced
- 1/2 cup red onion, finely chopped
- 1 cup shredded cheddar or Mexican blend cheese
- 2 cloves garlic, minced
- 1 teaspoon ground cumin
- 1 teaspoon chili powder
- 1/2 teaspoon paprika
- Salt and black pepper to taste
- Fresh cilantro or parsley for garnish (optional)
- Avocado slices for serving (optional)
- Lime wedges for serving (optional)

Instructions:

Preheat the oven to 375°F (190°C).
Place the halved bell peppers in a baking dish, cut side up.
In a large mixing bowl, combine cooked quinoa, black beans, corn, cherry tomatoes, red onion, shredded cheese, minced garlic, ground cumin, chili powder, paprika, salt, and black pepper. Mix well to combine.
Stuff each bell pepper half with the quinoa and black bean mixture, pressing it down slightly.
Cover the baking dish with aluminum foil and bake in the preheated oven for 25-30 minutes, or until the peppers are tender.
Remove the foil and bake for an additional 5-10 minutes, or until the cheese is melted and bubbly.
Optional: Garnish the stuffed peppers with fresh cilantro or parsley.
Serve the Quinoa and Black Bean Stuffed Peppers hot, optionally topped with avocado slices and lime wedges on the side.
Enjoy these nutritious and flavorful stuffed peppers as a wholesome and satisfying meal!

Fresh Herb Omelette

Ingredients:

- 3 large eggs
- 2 tablespoons milk or water
- 1 tablespoon butter or olive oil
- 2 tablespoons fresh chives, chopped
- 2 tablespoons fresh parsley, chopped
- 1 tablespoon fresh dill, chopped
- Salt and black pepper to taste
- Grated cheese (cheddar, feta, or your choice) - optional
- Sliced tomatoes or avocado for garnish - optional

Instructions:

In a bowl, whisk together the eggs, milk or water, chopped chives, parsley, and dill. Season with salt and black pepper.
Heat butter or olive oil in a non-stick skillet over medium-high heat until melted and hot.
Pour the egg mixture into the skillet, tilting the pan to ensure an even spread.
Allow the eggs to set around the edges. As they set, gently lift the edges with a spatula, tilting the pan to let the uncooked eggs flow to the edges.
Once the omelette is mostly set but still slightly runny on top, add any optional cheese to one half of the omelette.
Carefully fold the other half over the cheese, creating a half-moon shape.
Continue cooking for another minute or until the cheese is melted, and the omelette is cooked to your desired doneness.
Slide the omelette onto a plate.
Garnish with additional fresh herbs, sliced tomatoes, or avocado if desired.
Serve the Fresh Herb Omelette hot and enjoy a simple and flavorful breakfast or brunch!

Zucchini Noodles with Pesto

Ingredients:

For the Zucchini Noodles:

- 4 medium-sized zucchini, spiralized or julienned
- Salt for sprinkling

For the Pesto:

- 2 cups fresh basil leaves, packed
- 1/2 cup grated Parmesan cheese
- 1/2 cup pine nuts or walnuts
- 2 cloves garlic, minced
- 1/2 cup extra-virgin olive oil
- Salt and black pepper to taste
- Juice of 1 lemon (optional)

Optional Toppings:

- Cherry tomatoes, halved
- Extra Parmesan cheese
- Pine nuts or chopped walnuts

Instructions:

For the Zucchini Noodles:

Sprinkle salt over the zucchini noodles and let them sit in a colander for about 15-20 minutes. This helps draw out excess moisture.
After 15-20 minutes, rinse the salted zucchini noodles under cold water and pat them dry with a clean kitchen towel.

For the Pesto:

In a food processor, combine fresh basil, grated Parmesan cheese, pine nuts or walnuts, and minced garlic.
Pulse until the ingredients are finely chopped.
With the food processor running, gradually pour in the olive oil until the pesto reaches your desired consistency.
Season with salt and black pepper to taste. If you like, add a squeeze of lemon juice for extra brightness.

Assembling:

In a large mixing bowl, toss the spiralized or julienned zucchini noodles with the freshly made pesto until well coated.
Optional: Add cherry tomatoes, extra Parmesan cheese, and pine nuts or chopped walnuts for extra flavor and texture.
Serve the Zucchini Noodles with Pesto immediately, either as a light and refreshing main dish or as a side.
Enjoy this low-carb and flavorful alternative to traditional pasta!

Apple Cider Glazed Pork Chops

Ingredients:

- 4 bone-in pork chops
- Salt and black pepper to taste
- 2 tablespoons olive oil

For the Glaze:

- 1 cup apple cider
- 2 tablespoons Dijon mustard
- 2 tablespoons maple syrup
- 1 tablespoon apple cider vinegar
- 1 teaspoon cornstarch (optional, for thickening)

Instructions:

Preheat the oven to 375°F (190°C).
Season the pork chops with salt and black pepper on both sides.
In an oven-safe skillet, heat olive oil over medium-high heat.
Sear the pork chops for 3-4 minutes on each side, or until they develop a golden brown crust.
While the pork chops are searing, whisk together the apple cider, Dijon mustard, maple syrup, and apple cider vinegar in a bowl.
Pour the apple cider glaze over the seared pork chops in the skillet.
If desired, mix 1 teaspoon of cornstarch with a little water to create a slurry. Stir it into the glaze to thicken.
Transfer the skillet to the preheated oven and bake for 15-20 minutes, or until the pork chops reach an internal temperature of 145°F (63°C).
Baste the pork chops with the glaze during the last 5 minutes of baking.
Remove the skillet from the oven and let the pork chops rest for a few minutes before serving.
Spoon the apple cider glaze from the skillet over the pork chops.
Serve the Apple Cider Glazed Pork Chops hot, accompanied by your favorite side dishes.
Enjoy the delicious combination of savory pork and sweet apple cider glaze!

Roasted Tomato and Garlic Quiche

Ingredients:

For the Crust:

- 1 1/4 cups all-purpose flour
- 1/2 cup unsalted butter, cold and diced
- 1/4 teaspoon salt
- 2-3 tablespoons ice water

For the Filling:

- 1 pint cherry tomatoes, halved
- 1 head garlic, roasted
- 1 tablespoon olive oil
- 1 cup shredded Gruyere or Swiss cheese
- 4 large eggs
- 1 cup whole milk
- 1/2 cup heavy cream
- Salt and black pepper to taste
- Fresh basil or thyme for garnish

Instructions:

For the Crust:

> In a food processor, combine flour, diced cold butter, and salt. Pulse until the mixture resembles coarse crumbs.
> With the processor running, gradually add ice water until the dough comes together.
> Turn the dough onto a floured surface and shape it into a disk. Wrap in plastic wrap and refrigerate for at least 30 minutes.
> Preheat the oven to 375°F (190°C).
> Roll out the chilled dough on a floured surface and fit it into a tart or quiche pan. Trim the excess edges.
> Prick the bottom of the crust with a fork. Line the crust with parchment paper and fill it with pie weights or dried beans.

Bake the crust in the preheated oven for 15 minutes. Remove the parchment paper and weights, then bake for an additional 5 minutes until lightly golden. Set aside.

For the Filling:

Preheat the oven to 400°F (200°C).
Toss the halved cherry tomatoes with olive oil, salt, and pepper. Roast in the preheated oven for 20-25 minutes or until the tomatoes are slightly caramelized.
Squeeze the roasted garlic cloves out of the head.
In a bowl, whisk together eggs, whole milk, heavy cream, salt, and black pepper.
Spread the shredded cheese over the baked crust.
Arrange the roasted tomatoes and roasted garlic cloves over the cheese.
Pour the egg mixture over the tomatoes and garlic.
Reduce the oven temperature to 375°F (190°C) and bake the quiche for 30-35 minutes or until the center is set and the top is golden brown.
Allow the quiche to cool for a few minutes before slicing.
Garnish with fresh basil or thyme.
Serve the Roasted Tomato and Garlic Quiche warm or at room temperature.
Enjoy this flavorful and savory quiche as a delightful brunch or dinner option!

Grilled Eggplant with Tahini Dressing

Ingredients:

For the Grilled Eggplant:

- 2 large eggplants, sliced into rounds
- 3 tablespoons olive oil
- Salt and black pepper to taste
- 1 teaspoon ground cumin (optional)
- 1 teaspoon paprika (optional)

For the Tahini Dressing:

- 1/2 cup tahini
- 2 tablespoons lemon juice
- 2 tablespoons water
- 1 clove garlic, minced
- Salt to taste
- Fresh parsley, chopped, for garnish

Instructions:

For the Grilled Eggplant:

Preheat the grill or grill pan to medium-high heat.
In a bowl, toss the eggplant slices with olive oil, salt, black pepper, ground cumin, and paprika.
Grill the eggplant slices for about 3-4 minutes per side or until they are tender and have grill marks.

For the Tahini Dressing:

In a small bowl, whisk together tahini, lemon juice, water, minced garlic, and salt until smooth.
If the dressing is too thick, add more water until it reaches your desired consistency.

Assembling:

Arrange the grilled eggplant slices on a serving platter.
Drizzle the tahini dressing over the grilled eggplant.
Garnish with chopped fresh parsley.
Serve the Grilled Eggplant with Tahini Dressing as a delicious appetizer or side dish.
Enjoy the smoky flavor of the grilled eggplant paired with the creamy and tangy tahini dressing!

Cranberry Walnut Quinoa Salad

Ingredients:

- 1 cup quinoa, rinsed and cooked according to package instructions
- 1/2 cup dried cranberries
- 1/2 cup chopped walnuts, toasted
- 1/4 cup red onion, finely chopped
- 1/4 cup fresh parsley, chopped
- 1/4 cup feta cheese, crumbled
- Zest and juice of 1 lemon
- 3 tablespoons extra-virgin olive oil
- 1 tablespoon balsamic vinegar
- Salt and black pepper to taste
- Fresh arugula or mixed greens for serving (optional)

Instructions:

Cook the quinoa according to package instructions. Once cooked, let it cool to room temperature.

In a large bowl, combine the cooked quinoa, dried cranberries, toasted walnuts, chopped red onion, fresh parsley, and crumbled feta cheese.

In a separate small bowl, whisk together the olive oil, balsamic vinegar, lemon zest, and lemon juice.

Pour the dressing over the quinoa mixture and toss gently to combine.

Season the salad with salt and black pepper to taste. Adjust the seasoning if needed.

If desired, serve the Cranberry Walnut Quinoa Salad over a bed of fresh arugula or mixed greens.

Garnish with additional chopped parsley, cranberries, and walnuts.

Serve the salad immediately or refrigerate for later.

Enjoy this vibrant and nutritious salad as a refreshing side dish or a light and wholesome main course!

Garlic Parmesan Roasted Broccoli

Ingredients:

- 1 pound (about 450g) broccoli florets
- 3 tablespoons olive oil
- 4 cloves garlic, minced
- 1/3 cup grated Parmesan cheese
- 1 teaspoon lemon zest (optional)
- Salt and black pepper to taste
- Lemon wedges for serving (optional)

Instructions:

Preheat the oven to 425°F (220°C).
In a large bowl, toss the broccoli florets with olive oil, minced garlic, grated Parmesan cheese, lemon zest (if using), salt, and black pepper. Make sure the broccoli is evenly coated.
Spread the broccoli in a single layer on a baking sheet lined with parchment paper.
Roast in the preheated oven for 20-25 minutes, or until the broccoli is tender and the edges are slightly crispy.
While roasting, toss the broccoli halfway through the cooking time to ensure even roasting.
Remove from the oven and transfer the Garlic Parmesan Roasted Broccoli to a serving dish.
Optional: Squeeze fresh lemon juice over the top before serving for a burst of citrus flavor.
Serve the roasted broccoli hot as a delicious and flavorful side dish.
Enjoy the crispy and savory goodness of this Garlic Parmesan Roasted Broccoli!

Buttermilk Herb Roasted Chicken

Ingredients:

- 1 whole chicken (about 4-5 pounds)
- 2 cups buttermilk
- 3 cloves garlic, minced
- 1 tablespoon fresh rosemary, chopped
- 1 tablespoon fresh thyme leaves
- 1 tablespoon fresh parsley, chopped
- Zest and juice of 1 lemon
- Salt and black pepper to taste
- 2 tablespoons olive oil
- 1 onion, quartered
- 2 carrots, chopped
- 2 celery stalks, chopped

Instructions:

In a bowl, combine buttermilk, minced garlic, chopped rosemary, thyme, parsley, lemon zest, and lemon juice. Mix well.
Season the whole chicken with salt and black pepper, inside and out.
Place the chicken in a large resealable plastic bag or a marinating dish.
Pour the buttermilk mixture over the chicken, ensuring it's well-coated. Seal the bag or cover the dish and refrigerate for at least 4 hours or overnight.
Preheat the oven to 400°F (200°C).
Remove the chicken from the marinade, allowing any excess to drip off, but do not wipe off the herbs.
In a roasting pan, place the quartered onion, chopped carrots, and chopped celery. Drizzle with olive oil and season with salt and black pepper.
Place the marinated chicken on top of the vegetables.
Roast in the preheated oven for approximately 1 hour and 15 minutes, or until the internal temperature reaches 165°F (74°C) and the skin is golden brown and crispy.
Baste the chicken with the pan juices every 20-30 minutes for added flavor.
Once done, remove the Buttermilk Herb Roasted Chicken from the oven and let it rest for about 10 minutes before carving.
Serve the succulent roasted chicken with the flavorful vegetables on the side.

Enjoy the tender and juicy goodness of this Buttermilk Herb Roasted Chicken as a delightful main course!

Avocado and Tomato Salsa

Ingredients:

- 2 ripe avocados, diced
- 1 cup cherry tomatoes, halved
- 1/4 cup red onion, finely chopped
- 1/4 cup fresh cilantro, chopped
- 1 jalapeño, seeds removed and finely chopped (optional for heat)
- 1 clove garlic, minced
- Juice of 1 lime
- Salt and black pepper to taste

Instructions:

In a medium bowl, combine diced avocados, halved cherry tomatoes, chopped red onion, chopped cilantro, chopped jalapeño (if using), and minced garlic.
Squeeze the juice of one lime over the mixture.
Gently toss the ingredients together until well combined.
Season the salsa with salt and black pepper to taste. Adjust the seasoning as needed.
Allow the salsa to sit for a few minutes to let the flavors meld.
Serve the Avocado and Tomato Salsa immediately as a refreshing dip, topping for grilled proteins, or side for tacos and other dishes.
Enjoy the creamy avocado paired with the freshness of tomatoes in this vibrant and delicious salsa!

Ratatouille Stuffed Bell Peppers

Ingredients:

- 4 large bell peppers, halved and seeds removed
- 1 zucchini, diced
- 1 eggplant, diced
- 1 onion, finely chopped
- 2 tomatoes, diced
- 2 cloves garlic, minced
- 1/4 cup fresh basil, chopped
- 1/4 cup fresh parsley, chopped
- 1 teaspoon dried oregano
- Salt and black pepper to taste
- 2 tablespoons olive oil
- 1 cup cooked quinoa or rice (optional)
- Grated Parmesan cheese for topping (optional)

Instructions:

Preheat the oven to 375°F (190°C).
In a large skillet, heat olive oil over medium heat.
Add chopped onion and minced garlic to the skillet, sautéing until softened.
Add diced zucchini, diced eggplant, and diced tomatoes to the skillet. Cook for 5-7 minutes until the vegetables are tender.
Stir in fresh basil, fresh parsley, dried oregano, salt, and black pepper. Cook for an additional 2-3 minutes.
If using, mix in the cooked quinoa or rice to the vegetable mixture. Stir until well combined.
Place the halved bell peppers in a baking dish.
Spoon the ratatouille mixture into each bell pepper half, pressing it down gently.
Optionally, sprinkle grated Parmesan cheese over the top of each stuffed pepper.
Cover the baking dish with aluminum foil and bake in the preheated oven for 25-30 minutes, or until the peppers are tender.
Remove the foil and bake for an additional 5-7 minutes to allow the cheese to melt and slightly brown.
Serve the Ratatouille Stuffed Bell Peppers hot, garnished with extra fresh herbs if desired.

Enjoy these flavorful and colorful stuffed bell peppers as a satisfying and healthy meal!

Lemon Thyme Grilled Salmon

Ingredients:

- 4 salmon fillets
- Zest and juice of 1 lemon
- 2 tablespoons fresh thyme leaves, chopped
- 2 tablespoons olive oil
- 2 cloves garlic, minced
- Salt and black pepper to taste
- Lemon wedges for serving

Instructions:

In a small bowl, whisk together the lemon zest, lemon juice, chopped thyme, olive oil, minced garlic, salt, and black pepper to create the marinade.
Place the salmon fillets in a shallow dish or a zip-top bag.
Pour the marinade over the salmon, ensuring that each fillet is well-coated.
Marinate for at least 30 minutes in the refrigerator.
Preheat the grill to medium-high heat.
Remove the salmon from the marinade and let any excess drip off.
Place the salmon fillets on the preheated grill, skin side down. Grill for 4-5 minutes per side or until the salmon is cooked to your desired doneness.
While grilling, baste the salmon with the remaining marinade for added flavor.
Once done, remove the Lemon Thyme Grilled Salmon from the grill.
Serve the grilled salmon hot, garnished with extra fresh thyme and lemon wedges on the side.
Enjoy the bright and herby flavors of this delicious Lemon Thyme Grilled Salmon!

Roasted Brussels Sprouts with Cranberries

Ingredients:

- 1 pound Brussels sprouts, trimmed and halved
- 1/2 cup dried cranberries
- 2 tablespoons olive oil
- 2 tablespoons balsamic vinegar
- 1 tablespoon honey or maple syrup
- Salt and black pepper to taste
- 1/4 cup chopped pecans or walnuts (optional)

Instructions:

Preheat the oven to 400°F (200°C).
In a large mixing bowl, combine the halved Brussels sprouts and dried cranberries.
In a small bowl, whisk together olive oil, balsamic vinegar, honey or maple syrup, salt, and black pepper.
Pour the dressing over the Brussels sprouts and cranberries. Toss until the vegetables are evenly coated.
Spread the Brussels sprouts and cranberries in a single layer on a baking sheet.
Roast in the preheated oven for 20-25 minutes or until the Brussels sprouts are golden brown and crispy on the edges.
If using, sprinkle chopped pecans or walnuts over the top during the last 5 minutes of roasting.
Remove from the oven and transfer the Roasted Brussels Sprouts with Cranberries to a serving dish.
Serve the dish hot as a flavorful and festive side for any meal.
Enjoy the sweet and savory combination of roasted Brussels sprouts and cranberries!

Spaghetti Squash with Sage Brown Butter

Ingredients:

- 1 medium-sized spaghetti squash, halved and seeds removed
- 4 tablespoons unsalted butter
- 8-10 fresh sage leaves
- Salt and black pepper to taste
- Grated Parmesan cheese for garnish (optional)
- Chopped fresh parsley for garnish (optional)

Instructions:

Preheat the oven to 400°F (200°C).
Place the spaghetti squash halves, cut side down, on a baking sheet.
Roast in the preheated oven for 40-50 minutes or until the squash is fork-tender.
While the squash is roasting, prepare the sage brown butter. In a small saucepan over medium heat, melt the butter.
Once the butter is melted, add the fresh sage leaves. Allow them to cook in the butter until they become crispy, about 2-3 minutes. Be careful not to burn the butter; it should turn a golden brown color.
Remove the sage leaves from the butter and set them aside.
Once the spaghetti squash is done roasting, use a fork to scrape the flesh into strands.
Drizzle the sage brown butter over the spaghetti squash strands. Toss gently to coat.
Season with salt and black pepper to taste.
Garnish with the crispy sage leaves, grated Parmesan cheese, and chopped fresh parsley if desired.
Serve the Spaghetti Squash with Sage Brown Butter immediately as a delicious and low-carb alternative to traditional pasta.
Enjoy the rich and nutty flavor of the sage brown butter paired with the natural sweetness of spaghetti squash!

Grilled Peach and Arugula Salad

Ingredients:

- 4 ripe peaches, halved and pitted
- 6 cups arugula
- 1/2 cup feta cheese, crumbled
- 1/4 cup chopped mint leaves
- 1/4 cup balsamic glaze
- 2 tablespoons extra-virgin olive oil
- Salt and black pepper to taste
- Optional: 1/4 cup toasted pecans or walnuts

Instructions:

Preheat the grill to medium-high heat.
Brush the peach halves with a little olive oil to prevent sticking.
Grill the peaches, cut side down, for 2-3 minutes or until they have grill marks and are slightly caramelized.
Remove the grilled peaches from the heat and let them cool slightly.
In a large bowl, combine arugula, crumbled feta cheese, and chopped mint leaves.
Slice the grilled peaches and add them to the salad.
Drizzle extra-virgin olive oil and balsamic glaze over the salad.
Toss the salad gently to combine all the ingredients.
Season with salt and black pepper to taste.
Optional: Sprinkle toasted pecans or walnuts over the top for added crunch.
Serve the Grilled Peach and Arugula Salad immediately as a refreshing side dish or light main course.
Enjoy the delightful combination of sweet, savory, and peppery flavors in this vibrant salad!

Mushroom and Thyme Risotto

Ingredients:

- 1 1/2 cups Arborio rice
- 1/2 cup dry white wine
- 6 cups vegetable or chicken broth, kept warm
- 1 cup mushrooms, sliced (a mix of cremini, shiitake, or your choice)
- 1 onion, finely chopped
- 3 cloves garlic, minced
- 1/2 cup Parmesan cheese, grated
- 2 tablespoons unsalted butter
- 2 tablespoons olive oil
- 1 tablespoon fresh thyme leaves
- Salt and black pepper to taste
- Chopped fresh parsley for garnish (optional)

Instructions:

In a large skillet or saucepan, heat olive oil over medium heat. Add the chopped onion and sauté until translucent.
Add the minced garlic and cook for another 1-2 minutes until fragrant.
Stir in the Arborio rice and cook for 2-3 minutes, allowing the rice to toast slightly.
Pour in the white wine and cook until the wine is mostly absorbed by the rice.
Begin adding the warm broth, one ladle at a time, stirring frequently. Allow each addition of broth to be mostly absorbed before adding the next.
Continue this process until the rice is creamy and cooked to al dente, which will take about 18-20 minutes.
In a separate pan, heat butter over medium heat. Add the sliced mushrooms and cook until they are golden brown and any released liquid has evaporated.
Stir the cooked mushrooms into the risotto.
Add grated Parmesan cheese and fresh thyme leaves to the risotto. Stir well to combine.
Season with salt and black pepper to taste.
Optional: Garnish with chopped fresh parsley for a burst of color and freshness.
Serve the Mushroom and Thyme Risotto hot, and enjoy the rich, creamy goodness with the earthy flavors of mushrooms and thyme!

www.ingramcontent.com/pod-product-compliance
Lightning Source LLC
LaVergne TN
LVHW081318060526
838201LV00055B/2341